Panashe Blessing Muskwe

CHRISTIANITY
MODERN LIVING
& CONSUMERISM

FOLLOWING THE LORD'S WAY IN THESE DAYS OF
MATERIALISM AND THE PURSUIT OF WEALTH

Panashe Blessing Muskwe

CHRISTIANITY MODERN LIVING & CONSUMERISM

FOLLOWING THE LORD'S WAY IN THESE DAYS OF MATERIALISM AND THE PURSUIT OF WEALTH

MEREO

Mereo Books

2nd Floor, 6-8 Dyer Street, Cirencester, Gloucestershire, GL7 2PF Tel
An imprint of Memoirs Book Ltd. www.mereobooks.com

Christianity, Modern Living and Consumerism 978-1-86151-949-8

First published in Great Britain in 2019
by Mereo Books, an imprint of Memoirs Books Ltd.

The address for Memoirs Books Ltd. can be
found at www.memoirspublishing.com

Memoirs Books Ltd. Reg. No. 7834348

Typeset in 11/15pt Century Schoolbook
by Wiltshire Associates Ltd.
Printed and bound in Great Britain

Dedication

I dedicate this book to my late uncle, Reverend Nicholas Muskwe, who was brutally killed during the Zimbabwean War of Independence for his unwavering belief and faith in our Lord Jesus Christ. We still feel the loss and pain.

Contents

Preface

This book expresses the need for believers to remain steadfast in their faith and not to be carried away or vexed by the vicissitudes of modern-day life, consumerism and materialism, now that our modern way of life has increasingly become subverted by commercialisation and consumerism. Jesus Christ should be the centre of our world and at the heart of everything we do, and nothing in this materialistic world should stand in the way of our worshipping God, Lord Jesus. Earthly pleasures are temporal and not eternal, and must go the way of all flesh. In everyday life a Christian must pursue the path of honesty, diligence and humility, because the Lord prefers people who are humble and esteem others above themselves, and God above all.

We should always be mindful that the Devil now uses his wiles in the form of greed and unquenchable appetites for goods to entice us into debt and abnormal behaviour.

If we lose the truth that Jesus Christ is the centre of our world, materialism will continue to alienate us from His being and our purpose in life. The goods that we buy are only for our use and nothing more. They will never replace Christ. This book has been written to guide your way to a better life in God.

Acknowledgements

My deepest fond thanks go to my wife, Tasi Havazvidi, the girl from Masvingo who has been supportive to me through difficult and challenging times. I love you. Not forgetting my little pumpkins,Tawana and Munashe.

I also salute the Christian upbringing and values that I received from my parents, Mr Elliah Muyati Huntingfield Muskwe, who is now late, and my surviving mother, Mrs Bertha Kubvoruno Muskwe.

Special thanks go to my current Pastor, Trevor Nyamande, AFM Steven Assembly, for having taken time from his busy schedule to assist with the editing of this script. He continues to be a blessing to my family

The acknowledgments would not be complete without giving special thanks to my mothers in Christ, Apostle Merica Cox of Balm of Gilead World Ministries and Pastor Cecilia Dewu of On the Rock Ministries for teaching me how to pray and identifying my gift.

Introduction

Our current modern living, which has become overburdened and characterised by commercialisation and consumerism, has to a great extent obscured the Gospel and attempted to put it on the fringes of our everyday life. It has also influenced some Christians into believing that materialism has become the essence of living, thereby creating a false sense of security and purpose.

We should never forget that Jesus Christ should be the centre of our world and at the heart of everything we do. It is important for us to define who is a Christian. In simple parlance, a Christian is an individual who believes that Jesus Christ is Lord and that he died and rose again. Christians should also believe in the teachings of Jesus Christ, such as love, compassion and observing the statutes and commandments. The first people to be called Christians were believers at Antioch and who were seen to live like Christ.

The everyday life of a Christian needs to be embellished with honesty, diligence and humility. The Lord does not like haughty people; He prefers people who are humble and esteem others above themselves.

There has appeared an over-emphasis on materialism and a negation of the spiritual man. As we live each day as believers, we should constantly be aware that our life on earth is as delicate as morning dew and we may die any time. Apostle Paul, in the book of Colossians 3v2 states: *'**set your mind on the things above, not on the things that are on earth'**.* This means that we should never replace the importance and sanctity of our Lord with earthly goods and materials. These are temporal. Fashion comes and goes. There are always new gadgets each year, but there is only one God, Yeshua. We need to focus on things from above, not the things that are temporal and can easily vanish.

There is nothing wrong in liking nice cars, clothes, shoes and handbags, to name but a few material desires, but we should not forget the need for us to glorify our Lord and God and live by his word, commandments and statutes. The word of the Lord endures forever and is the same yesterday, today and tomorrow (Hebrews 13:8). No matter how busy our lives are, we should not forget to observe His ordinances, perform His requirements and meet His expectations.

Some past and present authors have questioned the existence of God, the Holy Spirit and Jesus Christ and have tried through their writings to obliterate our beliefs. But every believer must know that Jesus was the same yesterday as He will be tomorrow. He does not change, and his promises are yes and amen. (2 Corinthians 1:20).

The Word of the Lord and the Ten Commandments which were given to the prophet Moses at Mount Sinai define and clarify the expectations of Christian living in this modern-day world. God's word is true and does not change. The commandments that were given to Moses at Mount Sinai are still applicable today, for the Gospel endures forever.

The book of John v1-3 states*: 'In the beginning was the Word, and the Word was with God, and the Word was God.² He was in the beginning with God. ³ All things were made through Him, and without Him nothing was made that was made. ⁴ In Him was* *life, and the life was the light of men. ⁵ And the light shines in the darkness, and the darkness did not comprehend it.'*

It is important for us to understand that the commandments were created by God as a way of social control and can be argued to have been a precursor of many laws and edicts across the globe. The Word with regard to social justice and laws, provided a benchmark of what was accepted in the community or not.

Deuteronomy 11 vs 1 states: '***Therefore you shall love the Lord your God, and keep His charge, His statutes, His judgments, and His commandments always.'*** This verse highlights the importance of loving our Maker and the need to keep his commandments. It would be difficult for us to express love to our God, yet we do not keep His commandments or statutes.

There were benefits or blessings for following the law and curses for violating them. This is still relevant today and we should never fool ourselves by thinking that this only belonged to the Old Testament. Deuteronomy 12 v 26-29 : *²⁶Behold, I set before you today a blessing and a curse: ²⁷the blessing, if you obey the commandments of the Lord your God which I command you today; ²⁸and the curse, if you do not obey the commandments of the Lord your God, but turn aside from the way which I command you today, to go after other gods which you have not known'.*

We should always remember that the Lord Jesus Christ did not come to do away with or remove the Old Testament but to fulfil the laws. '*In the same way, let your light shine before men, that they may see your good deeds and glorify your Father in heaven. *[17]*Do not think that I have come to abolish the Law or the Prophets; I have not come to abolish them, but to fulfil them. *[18]*For I tell you truly, until heaven and earth pass away, not a single jot, not a stroke of a pen, will disappear from the Law until everything is accomplished*' (Matthew 5:17). Every decision that we make must be grounded in good measure and taking sight of our expectations in Jesus Christ of Nazareth.

Following the Commandments and God's laws is a matter of choice, or election. The acceptance of Jesus Christ should not be forced on people but that they should follow Him of their own volition or conviction. *'And he said unto them, In what place so ever ye enter into an house, there abide till ye depart from that place. *[11]*And whosoever shall not receive you, nor hear you, when ye depart thence, shake off the dust under your feet for a testimony against them. Verily I say unto you, It shall be more tolerable for*

Sodom and Gomorrha in the day of judgment, than for that city' (Matthew 10:14).

This is very different from other religions or cultures, where people are compelled or forced to follow the prescribed religion. Our Lord gave us choices, but we need to discern what is right or wrong and take into cognisance that there are always consequences for our actions. It is always salient to bear in mind that he is also a God who will pass the iniquities of parents to the third or fourth generation.

We are now fortunate to live under the new covenant of Grace. Living under Grace does not however give us the leeway to sin. The matter of Grace will be further explored and explained in the book.

Ricky Warren, the distinguished writer and evangelist, highlighted in his well-received book *The Purpose Driven Life* that the observance of the Ten Commandments could be seen as a litmus test for how Christians adhere strictly to the Gospel. For meaningful Christian living we need to continue to engage with the Ten Commandments as a guide to our living, but these are not to condemn us, but spur us onto a good life.

The Bible tells us that there is no more condemnation to those who are called by God for his purpose. (Romans 8:1).

Though we may falter in some ways, we need to know that the Grace of God is on hand to pick us up. The bible teaches that *'a righteous man falls seven times and rise again'* (Proverbs 24vs16). There is an old Chinese proverb that states, ***'Our greatest fear is not in never failing, but in not rising each time we fail.'*** We should never forget that due to his abundant mercies and Grace, He always helps us to pick ourselves when we fall in our Christian walk.

Just for us to remember what is required of us, I have included the Ten Commandments below which need to be observed and adhered to:

1   I am the Lord your God, who brought you out of the land of Egypt, out of the house of bondage. You shall have no other gods before Me.

2   You shall not make for yourself a carved image, or any likeness of anything that is in heaven above, or that is in the earth beneath, or that is in the water under the earth; you shall not bow down to them nor serve them. For I, the Lord your God, am a jealous God, visiting the iniquity of the fathers on the children to the third and fourth genera-tions of those who hate Me, but showing mercy

to thousands, to those who love Me and keep My Commandments.

3   You shall not take the name of the Lord your God in vain, for the Lord will not hold him guiltless who takes His name in vain.

4   Remember the Sabbath day, to keep it holy. Six days you shall labour and do all your work, but the seventh day is the Sabbath of the Lord your God. In it you shall do no work: you, nor your son, nor your daughter, nor your male servant, nor your female servant, nor your cattle, nor your stranger who is within your gates. For in six days the Lord made the heavens and the earth, the sea, and all that is in them, and rested the seventh day. Therefore the Lord blessed the Sabbath day and hallowed it.

5   Honour your father and your mother, that your days may be long upon the land which the Lord your God is giving you.

6   You shall not murder.

7   You shall not commit adultery.

8   You shall not steal.

9   You shall not bear false witness against your neighbour.

10   You shall not covet your neighbour's house; you shall not covet your neighbour's wife, nor his male servant, nor his female servant, nor his ox, nor his donkey, nor anything that is your neighbour's.

1 Peter 1 vs 15 provides a clear call for Christians to live holy lives.We should not give in to advertisements that try to lure us into sexual immorality, greed, perversions, idle talk and sin. All things were created by God for our benefit and we should never let them profane us. We need to guard our hearts and minds vigilantly.

Philippians 4:7 states: *'And the peace of God, which passeth all understanding, shall keep your hearts and your minds through Christ Jesus'*. Our hearts need to be kept pure and holy for his sake. Proverbs 4:23 encourages us to 'Keep your heart with all diligence, for out of it are the issues of life.'

The computer age that we are living in and our modern inventions, goods and services are all subject to God. Colossians 1:16-17: *'As for by him were all things created, that are in heaven, and that are in earth, visible and invisible, whether they be thrones, or dominions, or principalities, or powers: all things were created by him, and for him:*[17] *'And he is before all things, and by him all things are held together'.*

These verses highlight the greatness, invincibility and magnanimity of our Lord. The clothes and the products that we wear should not replace and be equated to Jesus Christ.

Whatever man has created, God has given the wisdom and guidance.

As Christians we need to remain steadfast and continue to live according to His laws and expectations. We should never forget that devils come in sheep's clothing and that their purpose is to deceive us. It is also salient for us to be able to stand against consumerism, the information, practices and advertisements that go against our beliefs and views.

Chapter 1:

Media and Body Image

Current advertisements in the media propagate what some individuals in this country describe as acceptable or beautiful bodies. These advertisements usually show the bodies of women, often scantily dressed, of size 10 or below and tall. Their appearance is presented as ideal, and anyone who deviates too far from this appearance is observed or described as ugly. Being obese is like reading a book off the script.

With regards to men, a muscular physique and a 'six pack' is presented as the ideal body. This media approach has put much pressure on some individuals in society and has resulted in some taking slimming tablets or other concoctions and going under the knife, all in the name of having a good perceived image. We have allowed society to give us a narrative of how we ought to look, rather than looking unto Jesus the author and the finisher of our faith. Jesus Christ is the one who has the correct template of how we are made to look.

Continued exposure to an advertisement usually results in persuading many people to buy the product. This is the technique that Goebbels used in spreading Nazi propaganda during the Second World War. Continued exposure breeds familiarity and has social influence on us. This is the trick that the devil uses through the media. There are stories of adults and young people who have sustained fatal injuries or irreparable damage due to botched operations. Some have travelled to far-away countries for cosmetic surgery which ended up in disaster.

Some people suffering from anorexia nervosa as a result of trying to fit an image portrayed by the media. Anorexia nervosa is a serious mental health condition, an eating disorder where a person is obsessed with keeping their body weight as low as possible regardless of the consequences to their health. Some have become so emaciated that they have died or had to be admitted to hospital.

It is appropriate to mention that we should all aspire to have healthy bodies but not allow society to dictate to us how we should look and present. If we succumb to the pressure of society and individuals in defining how we look, then we are not abiding by the word of God.

The bible tells us that King David, who the God of Heaven described as a man after his heart in Psalm 139:14 said '*I praise you because I am fearfully and wonderfully made: your works are wonderful, I know that full well'.* If we are wonderfully and fearfully made as the Bible says, we should not allow society to give us a negative view of ourselves. We should walk tall and soar like eagles, looking down with confidence.

I was still young in my Christian walk when I first heard this verse being preached. The preacher was of small stature, possibly five feet in height, yet he said that he did not feel intimidated by people who were taller than him as he is a product of the works of God and no one should look down on him. This resonated with me and gave me so much confidence, as I was feeling confused by a number of events that were happening in my life and my self-confidence and efficacy had started to be compromised.

What I failed to understand at the time was that, I was made in the image of God and that no problems or issues would sublime me. I had forgotten that I was secure, unconquerable and enduring as mount Zion. **Psalm 125:1 'Those who trust in the LORD are like Mount Zion, which cannot be moved, but abides forever.'**

What we need to continuously bear in mind is that we are made in the image of God. What God has made is true, beautiful and good. Psalm 82:6 states: 'You are gods, you are all sons of the most high.' How then can gods be coerced or negatively influenced? Lack of awareness, gullibility and not being filled with the spirit renders us powerless and clueless. As Christians we are not at times conscious of our inheritance and the power that is contained within us. This is the power that rose our Lord from the grave. Apostle Paul mentions in **Philippians 3:10: 'That I may know him, and the power of his resurrection, and the fellowship of his sufferings, being made conformable unto his death.'** Hosea goes further in 4:6 to say: ' **My people are destroyed for lack of knowledge; because you have rejected knowledge, I reject you from being a priest** *to me. And since you have forgotten the law of your God, I also will forget your children'.*

There is no question that as Christians we are stewards of our bodies and that we need to guard and take care of them jealously and vigilantly, as they are the temple of the Lord. It is important that we are not overweight, as this brings its own health problems such as diabetes and heart disease and many other problems. It would not be appropriate to pray for weight loss, as we can easily change our lifestyles and eat healthily. Some changes come only as a way of making positive life choices. It is however of paramount importance that our motivation to change is noble and not to simply fit in to some societal expectations in order to feel accepted.

Chapter 2:

Sexualised Behaviour

It is worth mentioning that some of the advertisements on television and social media are very sexualised and sickening. They usually feature models who are semi-clad and with most of their flesh visible. Some of the advertisements also simulate sexual intercourse and make inappropriate sounds. There is a popular saying in marketing circles that 'sex sells'.

But what is surprising is that even some of the advertisements for commodities such as rice and ice cream are being sexualised. This continued exposure affects both the young and old and may end up believing what they see.

These advertisements take the same approach as propaganda that is used by politicians. The more people get exposed to a product, the greater the chance that they will buy into it. This is the essence of sales and marketing. As previously mentioned in the preceding pages this is the method that Goebbels used to hood wink the German public in believing his propaganda. This resulted in the murder and execution of vulnerable and defenceless Jews. The white supremacists in the United States of America and South Africa have and are still using the media to spread their propaganda that people of African heritage are cursed and inferior.

There are some dating sites which even encourage married people to be involved in illicit affairs. They advertise affairs as if they are something magical or special. We as believers should not fool ourselves, as our Lord Jesus Christ is vehemently against such practices.

The bible is clear that fornicators and adulterers will not inherit the Kingdom of Heaven.

Galatian 5 vs 19-21 states: *19 The acts of the flesh are obvious: sexual immorality, impurity and debauchery; 20 idolatry and witchcraft; hatred,*

discord, jealousy, fits of rage, selfish ambition, dissensions, factions 21 and envy; drunkenness, orgies, and the like. I warn you, as I did before, that those who live like this will not inherit the kingdom of God.

For parents there is a greater need to continue to affirm the best of their children so as to boost their confidence helps to arrest the need for cosmetic alteration of appearance to satisfy the unreal standards of society.

Children need to feel loved and appreciated. The world that our children are living in has become too sexualised, and the media and societal pressures have been the two main negative influences. This has not just been a modern phenomenon but is embedded in historic.

Bishop Tudor Bismarck wrote in the book *The Kingdom in Motion*. In the book, Caesarea Philippi was a beautiful place but filled with pagan worship. There was a Greek deity called Pan who was known as the God of sexual perversion and depravity. Pan was half man, half goat and was seen as the region's tribute to homosexuality, and this was also a place of orgies. Some Christians are now involved in sexual immorality due to societal pressures and influences.

In the modern age, there are some societies where it is now considered normal for a married man to have a girlfriend, who is called a 'small house', 'side chick' or 'the other woman'. This goes against what the bible teaches us about faithfulness and commitment. Married Christians should not be involved in extramarital affairs. Sexual intercourse is a treasure in marriage and should not be shared with anyone other than married partners.

Such liberal and inhibited sexual behaviour have led to the spreading of sexually-transmitted infections, including HIV/AIDS. There is also an issue of objectification of women in some advertisements. They are portrayed as objects of desire, and this can be argued as lessening or demeaning the role and social standing of women in the society. This point has been an argument put forward by feminists for a long time, and strong advocacy and protests are needed to eradicate such advertisements.

There is a need to educate children about relationships so as to ensure that they are enlightened. The Bible prohibits any sexual intercourse or any bodily contact between a man and a woman before they are married. There is no such thing as cohabiting in the Word. This is fornication. We need to walk in the spirit and not the flesh.

1 Corinthians 6:18: '***Flee fornication. Every sin that a man doeth is without the body, but he that committeth fornication sinneth against his own body'***. When a man commits adultery he will have shown covetousness towards someone's wife. In Exodus 20 v 17, it is written: '***You shall not covet your neighbour's house. You shall not covet your neighbour's wife, or his male or female servant, his ox or donkey, or anything that belongs to your neighbour.***'

The bible tells us that we should not conform to this world but that we must be steadfast in our beliefs. When we conform we lose the essence of who we are in Jesus Christ, a royal priesthood, a peculiar people.

Royals do not conform to the lives of commoners or society but are rather pace-setters. They usually stick to their traditions, beliefs and aspirations. For example the British Royal family always attend a church service together on Christmas Day. The members do not choose to go away on holiday during the Christmas period but spend time together. They have money to go on the most luxurious holidays, but elect not to. What makes royalty stand out is their tradition. Modernity does not mean getting rid of traditional beliefs, but must build on this.

Chapter 3:

Vanity and Plastic Surgery

Some individuals, due to social and family pressures in the world, have resorted to plastic surgery. This may include nose reconstruction, facial changes or uplifts. It is sad that some individuals no longer want to reveal their natural looks but have resorted to this. The number of people who have gone under the knife to have cosmetic surgery is ever increasing. Some have suffered from botched operations, and this has caused much physical and emotional distress.

The celebrity culture in the world today has led to some members of society wishing to look exactly like their heroes. In the United Kingdom, there was a case in the newspapers of a young man who spent a fortune in cosmetic surgery wanting to look like a certain glamour model. Without being critical of this young person, this shows the extent of how the celebrity culture has influenced the thinking of young people and society at large.

Do not look down upon yourself but be brave, be resolute like the Hebrew boys. They were subject to these horrifying experiences because they refused to bow down to the Kings' decrees or edicts that went against the beliefs of God and would not hero-worship the King. As a result of their beliefs and principles, they could not take any action that could compromise the gospel. They had been brought up knowing their God, Jehovah, and they would not compromise their views. This is the evidence of the teaching that had been instilled in them, which echoes Proverbs 22 v6: *'Train up a child in the way he should go, And when he is old he will not depart from it'.* These boys remained steadfast and fervent in prayer. Such resolve is needed in society today in the face of the pressures under discussion. Daniel 3 vs 16- 18 state: *'Shadrach, Meshach and Abednego, answered and said to the king, O Nebuchadnezzar, we are not careful to answer thee in this matter.*

17 If it be so, our God whom we serve is able to deliver us from the burning fiery furnace, and he will deliver us out of thine hand, O king.

18 But if not, be it known unto thee, O king, that we will not serve thy gods, nor worship the golden image which thou hast set up.'

We are a chosen generation of royal priesthood and should not be coerced into things that are against the teaching of the Word of God and our beliefs. All the media advertisements are gimmicks that are designed to try to influence our thinking and belief systems. The same can be argued as to when the Devil tried to tempt Jesus with earthly possessions after he had fasted for forty days and forty nights. Jesus at this time was hungry and weary. (Matthew 4:4-11). But he did not flinch or give in to the devil's temptations. Just imagine the gold and all the wealth of this word that Jesus was offered by Satan and refused. If he had been of a corrupt nature, he would have given in, but he remained steadfast to his principles and beliefs.

In Matthew 4:4-11: **4 Then Jesus was led by the Spirit into the wilderness to be tempted[a] by the devil. 2 After fasting forty days and forty nights, he was** hungry. ³ The tempter came to him and said, "If you are the Son of God, tell these stones to become bread."

⁴ Jesus answered, "It is written: 'Man shall not live on bread alone, but on every word that comes from the mouth of God.'[b]"

⁵ Then the devil took him to the holy city and had him stand on the highest point of the temple. ⁶ "If you are the Son of God," he said, "throw yourself down. For it is written:

"'He will command his angels concerning you, and they will lift you up in their hands, so that you will not strike your foot against a stone.'[c]"

⁷ Jesus answered him, "It is also written: 'Do not put the Lord your God to the test.'[d]"

⁸ Again, the devil took him to a very high mountain and showed him all the kingdoms of the world and their splendor. ⁹ "All this I will give you," he said, "if you will bow down and worship me."

¹⁰ Jesus said to him, "Away from me, Satan! For it is written: 'Worship the Lord your God, and serve him only.'[e]"

¹¹ Then the devil left him, and angels came and attended him.

Apostle Paul encourages us in 2 Corinthians 4 vs 18 that what we see is temporal but what we do not see is spiritual and eternal.

Beauty has nothing to do with race. Individuals need to be confident and celebrate their beauty, race or ethnicity. Whilst a past survey in the Metro newspaper indicated that most men who were asked about how they described a beautiful woman described their ideal as slim and tall with blonde hair. This is understandable, given that Britain is predominantly white British in terms of race.

Esther 1 v 10 says*: 'On the seventh day, when the heart of the King was merry with wine, he commanded Mehuman, Biztha, Harbona, Bigtha, Abagtha, Zotha and Carcas, the seven eunuchs who served in the presence of King Ahasurus, to bring Queen Vashti before the King, wearing her royal crown, in order to show her beauty to the people and officials, for she was beautiful to behold'*. Queen Vashti was of Persian origin and is unlikely to have had blue eyes or blonde hair. Queen Esther, who took over from Queen Vashti, was of Jewish origin and most likely did not have blue eyes. They were both however very beautiful and attractive. Individuals should cherish how they look and not to try to compare with someone as God created us differently.

There is a cultural element when it comes to beauty. In some African countries, like Zimbabwe, women who are well-built and curvaceous but not overweight are described as beautiful. Jennifer Lopez, the Spanish American celebrity, is described as beautiful by a number of newspapers and the media, but she is not of slim build; she has curves.

Some women have suffered severe skin burns and even life-changing disfigurement as a result of using bleaching liquids to make themselves look more fair-skinned. This can be argued from an African perspective to be a colonial hangover, because in colonial times people with lighter skins were seen to be superior and more acceptable in the community. Apartheid was a system that was practised in the US and some parts of Africa such as Zimbabwe and South Africa, which included the separation of services for blacks from those for whites based on the colour of their skin. So people of African origin or descent ended up receiving inferior services.

There was a cosmetic sold in Zimbabwe AMBI which affected the skins of a number of women in that country. Some political people interpreted the acronym as standing for Africans Must Be Improved.

As Christians, we need to guard our minds and

ensure that we are not unduly influenced by the media. There are also some people who have gone to great lengths to try to fit in the culture of the workplace.

I remember a time when I was working for a certain employer where there was a culture of swearing. Some would take the name of Christ in vain. Other workers, instead of challenging the practice, ended up swearing and making lewd jokes. I would ask them not to swear, as it was not appropriate behaviour in the workplace. Some started to call me names, but they avoided swearing in my presence. This highlights that human beings have a desire to belong to a group. I have noticed that some individuals are afraid to be labelled deviants or outcasts, as this would mean they do not belong to a group. Yet we always need to remember that we are not of this world, that our Kingdom is not of this world, but that of Heaven.

God tells us that we need to be the light and the salt of the earth. How can we be the light if we have succumbed to the wills of the world and ending up exuding darkness and filth? Our conduct should be exemplary and no fault should be in us. Jesus Christ requires a bride with no wrinkles and faults. We need to take a stand and let a no mean no and a yes mean yes. We should be bold and not be caught up in unholy discussions or unholy office banter. If we deny Him in public, He will also deny us in public.

Chapter 4:

Materialism and Christianity – the Protestant Ethic

We live in a world that has become much more materialistic and less human. It is now an upheld notion that the richer you are and the more possessions you have, the more respect and recognition you will get. But this should not be the situation. A person must be respected regardless of his or her possessions or how much money he or she has. The Bible mentions that the views of a poor man are not respected, but those of a rich man are. A failure to depart from this path means that the views, ideas and insights of a wide population will be lost.

A number of believers have found themselves in debt whilst trying to keep up appearances, or, as they say, 'keeping up with the Joneses.' The latest statistics highlight the fact that British household debt has surpassed the one trillion pound mark. This cuts across the board between Christians and non-Christians. Some have resorted to using credit cards to pay for their holidays and other luxuries that they cannot afford. Some have store cards for clothing which have skyrocketed out of control with regard to the money that has to be repaid. This has led to a number of people not being able to meet their repayments, and some have even filed for bankruptcy.

I have observed some families that have acquired very luxurious cars on hire purchase or credit whilst they are already struggling with debt. Some people on modest incomes go on to buy expensive items just to present an image that they are doing well financially. But it is important for families to stick to their budgets and not be influenced by advertisements or peer pressure into impulse buying. Lack of good budgeting has led to a lot of unbearable stress on marriage and individuals. This has led to many families having poor credit and even losing their homes.

Some people have even turned to crime for the purpose of amassing wealth and living lives that they cannot afford. Some are involved in fraud, embezzlement and misappropriation of funds. Headlines have appeared in newspapers about people of faith who have been arrested and sent to prison because of financial misappropriation. Yet among the Ten Commandments is one which states, 'thou shalt not steal'.

The current drugs problem in the world can be attributed to greed and selfishness. The drug barons are willing to use young children and see many people be addicted so as they make profit and increase their pockets. A lot of people have died in drugs wars between the militias of the barons and the police, especially in Colombia. Some police officers and judges have also been targeted and killed during these wars. Above all, families have been ruined and societies have been greatly affected. Some of these drug barons describe themselves as Catholics and philanthropists!

The devil snares you, then leaves you and humiliates you in the end. The power of enticement should not be understated. Jesus Christ was tempted with splendour by the devil in Matthew 4. Matthew 4 v1: *'Then Jesus was led by the Spirit into wilderness to be tempted by the devil. After fasting for forty days and forty nights, he was hungry. The tempter came to him and said 'If you are the Son of God, tell these stones to become bread'. Jesus answered, 'It is written: 'Man shall not live on bread alone, but on every word that comes from the mouth of God.'*

Verse 8-11: *'Again, the devil took him to a very high mountain and showed him all the kingdoms of the world and their splendour. 'All this I give you' he said, 'if you will bow down and worship me.' Jesus said to him 'Away from me, Satan. For it is written 'Worship the Lord your God and serve him only'. Then the devil left him, and angels came and attended him.'*

It is important and salient that as Christians we know the Word and are able to use it when difficult times come. We should not be weekend worshippers or lukewarm Christians. We should be able to say 'It is written', and quote the scriptures. For the Christian the importance of knowing the Word of God cannot be overemphasised.

There is no need for us to fret or be coerced into situations due to pressure. This can be viewed as destructive obedience. The psychologists gave the example of how the troops of Saddam Hussein used to follow orders unreservedly which involved killing and maiming the Kurdish population. This can paradoxically be likened to our lives when we follow other's views, opinions and pressures. We need to be stable and not be like Reuben, who the bible describes as being as unstable as the waters. Genesis 49:3-5:

"Reuben, you are my firstborn

My might and the beginning of my strength,

Preeminent in dignity and preeminent in power.

[4]"Uncontrolled as water, you shall not have pre-eminence, Because you went up to your father's bed; then you defiled it—he went up to my couch."

This was the time when Jacob had sat down to bless his sons before his death. I think Reuben thought he was going to receive a double portion of blessings as he was the firstborn. Jewish custom and society at that time favoured the firstborn, who usually ended up inheriting a big portion of the family's wealth. This however turned to be different for Reuben as a result of his actions. He had slept with his father's concubine, and this was an abhorrent crime. I am surprised he was not put to death at that time, but I put this down to the affection and love of his father. This account, in the book of Genesis, teaches us to pray and ask God for wisdom in making our decisions. If your decision-making is shaky you are likely to falter or stumble and not succeed.

In one of his sermons, TD Jakes gave an interesting analogy, saying that water takes the shape of any vessel that you put it in, whether it is a cup or a plastic bottle.

We need to know the hope of our calling and look forward towards Yahweh. This is where we need to recite or sing the song that says (to give a few verses):

Our God He lives forever

He reigns with power and love

Let earth bow down before Him

For He is exalted

We look to Yahweh, Yahweh

Forever Yahweh, Yahweh, oh, yeah

Our hope is God almighty

His love is Greater than all

Lift high the God of heaven

Give all the honour

We look to Yahweh, Yahweh

Our hope is Yahweh, Yahweh, yeah

And He shall reign forever

He shall reign forever

He shall reign forever and ever

And He shall reign forever

He shall reign forever

He shall reign forever and ever

Our God, yeah

We look to Yahweh, Yahweh Forever Yahweh, Yahweh

We look to Yahweh, Yahweh

Our hope is Yahweh, Yahweh.

It is important to include God in our endeavours and to know that he has a desired plan for us. Jeremiah 29 v 11 states this in very clear terms: ***"For I know the plans I have for you,"*** declares the Lord, ***"plans to prosper you and not to harm you, plans to give you hope and a future."*** This verse should bring much confidence and exuberance to our faith. We have a high God who is always interceding for us. We do not need to go out of our way to please people or to live up to someone's standards. The Lord also says in Isaiah 49:16: **'See, I have engraved you on the palms of my hands; your walls are ever before me'.**

The late Muhammad Ali, born Cassius Marcellus Clay Jnr, never ceased to amaze me about his resolve and principle. He fiercely criticised the war in Vietnam and was called for duty by the American government and refused. He knew what was at stake; he could go to prison and lose his heavyweight championship medals, belts and sponsorship. Yet he continued to criticise the war. He was subsequently imprisoned and his championship belts taken away from him. It should go without saying that Muhammad Ali was influential in mobilising resistance against the war in Vietnam, as well as the black civil rights movement. This is the kind of courage we need to have and admire. As Christians we also need to be resolute in our beliefs and faith.

No one ever thought that Barack Obama would become the first African-American President of the United States of America when he started to campaign in the primaries against the former First Lady of the United States of America. He won against Hillary Clinton and later triumphed against John McCain, the Republican nominee. Obama's self-confidence and self-belief propelled him to great heights against all odds. He used his eloquence mass mobilising skills to propel him to victory.

Gideon had a poor image and self-esteem but believed in God. He was called a 'mighty man of valour' by an angel, though he was fearful and fretful in spirit.

Judges 6vs 11-23 states: *'And there came an angel of the LORD, and sat under an oak which was in Ophrah, that pertained unto Joash the Abiezrite: and his son Gideon threshed wheat by the winepress, to hide it from the Midianites. 12And the angel of the LORD appeared unto him, and said unto him, The LORD is with thee, thou mighty man of valour. 13And Gideon said unto him, Oh my Lord, if the LORD be with us, why then is all this befallen us? and where be all his miracles which our fathers told us of, saying, Did not the LORD bring us up from Egypt? but now the LORD hath forsaken us, and delivered us into the hands of the Midianites. 14And the LORD looked upon him, and said, Go in this thy might, and thou shalt save Israel from the hand of the Midianites: have not I sent thee? 15And he said unto him, Oh my Lord, wherewith shall I save Israel? behold, my family is poor in Manasseh, and I am the least in my father's house. 16And the LORD said unto him, Surely I will be with thee, and thou shalt smite the Midianites as one man.*

[17]And he said unto him, If now I have found grace in thy sight, then shew me a sign that thou talkest with me. [18]Depart not hence, I pray thee, until I come unto thee, and bring forth my present, and set it before thee. And he said, I will tarry until thou come again.

[19]And Gideon went in, and made ready a kid, and unleavened cakes of an ephah of flour: the flesh he put in a basket, and he put the broth in a pot, and brought it out unto him under the oak, and presented it. [20]And the angel of God said unto him, Take the flesh and the unleavened cakes, and lay them upon this rock, and pour out the broth. And he did so. [21]Then the angel of the LORD put forth the end of the staff that was in his hand, and touched the flesh and the unleavened cakes; and there rose up fire out of the rock, and consumed the flesh and the unleavened cakes. Then the angel of the LORD departed out of his sight. [22]And when Gideon perceived that he was an angel of the LORD, Gideon said, Alas, O Lord GOD! for because I have seen an angel of the LORD face to face. [23]And the LORD said unto him, Peace be unto thee; fear not: thou shalt not die."

In this world, we should always be in a position to stand up and achieve our calling and not be cowed by the world but stand up on the word. If Gideon had not had courage and belief in the Lord, he might not have been involved in saving his community from the Midianites. Up until this time, the Israelites had been resigned to the fact that the Midianites would persistently come and loot and plunder Israelites' livestock and crops.

Only one man had to heed the call of God and defend his people, and that man was Gideon. Public opinion and negative or opposing voices could not hold him back. This is what we should do every time, to stand up against the dark forces in the society, which include those of consumerism.

We need to stand in unison and proclaim that we and our children will not be influenced by the invasive and voracious advertisements on television. As the children of promise, we need to keep on reminding ourselves that we have a high God who keeps on making intercession for us. In making this declaration, we need to assert that despite the media's influence, we and our families have the resolve to stand against the devil's wiles that are masquerading as consumerism and modernisation.

Matthew 6 v24 states: *'No man can serve two masters: for either he will hate the one, and love the other; or else he will hold to the one, and despise the other. Ye cannot serve God and mammon.'* Mammon refers to the world economic systems and the wealth of nations. This also includes greed and evil worship of money.

The problems in the banking sector and the onset of recession in 2008 in the United Kingdom and the United States was closely linked to the selling of subprime mortgages. A subprime mortgage is a type of loan granted to individuals with poor credit scores (640 or less, and often below 600), who, as a result of their deficient credit histories, would not be able to qualify for conventional mortgages. Big banks such as Lehman Brothers were involved in the selling of subprime mortgages, as they were making a lot of profit on interest. The problems started to show when a number of mortgagees started to default on their payments and this compounded and was a factor in causing the financial crisis. These problems might have been avoided if greed and the desire for extreme profiteering. The recession showed that the world economy is fragile and cannot be trusted.

We should always trust Jesus Christ, as He is the

panacea to all our problems and challenges. He is the one who brings financial prosperity and sustenance. In Deuteronomy 8:18, God tells us that he is the one who gives us the power to make wealth. All the wealth in the world belongs to him.

The over-dependence on the economy can be attributed to capitalism, which dictates that the people's needs and provision should be through the labour market. This has however not been the case, as inflation has generally outstripped pay increases.

It is important to note that capitalism, like communism and socialism, has failed to meet the needs of the general public and has rather been exacerbating the inequalities between the rich and the poor due to greed and self-gratification. The report by Crédit Suisse (2017) highlights that the globe's richest 1% own half the world's wealth, there is also growing gap between the super-rich and everyone else. The world's richest people are reported to have seen their share of the globe's total wealth increase from 42.5% at the height of the 2008 financial crisis to 50.1% in 2017, or $140tn (£106tn), according to Credit Suisse's global wealth report. These figures show the amount of greed across the world and how only a small elite can end up controlling it.

Greed, drugs and prostitution

The current drug problem in the world is the result of greed and self-aggrandisement. It is important to highlight the fact that a number of people have died as a result of drug use and drug wars. In Latin America, especially in Colombia and Mexico, the governments have been struggling to fight the drug lords and to quell the drugs trade. There have been street battles between the government forces and the drug militia. Most people are aware of Pablo Escobar, the drug lord originally from Medellin in Colombia, who is reported to have caused a lot of deaths through his activities. Escobar's career ended when he was shot dead in a gun battle with police in 1993.

It is estimate that the international drug trade is worth more than £300 billion and growing. The opium fields of Afghanistan are expanding and drugs such as cocaine, heroin and cannabis are now being sold on the streets in many countries. This problem has been compounded by the poverty that most pedlars suffer, which leads to them being drawn into the drug trade.

Many children across the world live in abject poverty and some are forced into prostitution. This makes them vulnerable to sexual exploitation and significant harm.

They can never realise their dreams and aspirations, despite the great wealth across the world and the United Nations protocols which are meant to protect them.

The great inequality between the rich and poor has been widening and there are few opportunities for self-realisation for the needy. We live in a war that is characterised by wars and refugee movements – human suffering.

Believers need to pray for peace and love to prevail on earth. It is morally wrong for individuals to dwell in splendour and riches while we have children living in abject poverty and deprivation. We should be minded to love one another as Christ loved the church.

Jesus Christ in John 15 vs 12 stated: *'This is my commandment, that you love one another as I have loved you.'* We can show our love by sharing our possessions and wealth with those in need. The essence of sharing wealth as a way of providing for need is highlighted in the Book of Acts. Acts 4 vs 34-35 says: '*Nor was there anyone among them who lacked; for all who were possessors of houses sold them, and brought the proceeds of the things that were sold, and laid them on the apostle's feet, and they distributed to each as anyone had need'.*

There should not be anyone who should suffer poverty in the church as we are all 'my brother's keeper'. This is not to coerce or to manipulate people into selling their assets to assist the needy, but we should look after one another and always show love and affection to the brethren.

It also needs to be acknowledged that greed is now a feature of some clergy. We have heard stories of some clergy telling their church members that if they buy and use the armbands and the oil that they have prayed for, they will be cured of diseases and have financial good fortune. God's power cannot be confined to material things and manipulation. The story of Gehazi in 2 Kings 5 highlights that greed is not only confined to the word but also to the house of God.

2 Kings vs 1-26: *'1 Now Naaman, captain of the host of the king of Syria, was a great man with his master, and honorable, because by him Jehovah had given victory unto Syria: he was also a mighty man of valor, but he was a leper. 2 And the Syrians had gone out in bands, and had brought away captive out of the land of Israel a little maiden; and she waited on Naaman's wife. 3 And she said unto her mistress, Would that my lord were with the prophet that is in Samaria! then would he recover him of his leprosy.*

4And one went in, and told his lord, saying, Thus and thus said the maiden that is of the land of Israel. 5And the king of Syria said, Go now, and I will send a letter unto the king of Israel. And he departed, and took with him ten talents of silver, and six thousand pieces of gold, and ten changes of raiment.

6 And he brought the letter to the king of Israel, saying, And now when this letter is come unto thee, behold, I have sent Naaman my servant to thee, that thou mayest recover him of his leprosy. 7 And it came to pass, when the king of Israel had read the letter, that he rent his clothes, and said, Am I God, to kill and to make alive, that this man doth send unto me to recover a man of his leprosy? but consider, I pray you, and see how he seeketh a quarrel against me.

8 And it was so, when Elisha the man of God heard that the king of Israel had rent his clothes, that he sent to the king, saying, Wherefore hast thou rent thy clothes? let him come now to me, and he shall know that there is a prophet in Israel. 9 So Naaman came with his horses and with his chariots, and stood at the door of the house of Elisha. 10 And Elisha sent a messenger unto him, saying, Go and wash in the Jordan seven times, and thy flesh shall come again to thee, and thou shalt be clean. 11 But Naaman was wroth, and went away, and said, Behold, I thought, He will surely come out to me, and stand, and call on the name of Jehovah his God, and wave his hand over the place, and recover the leper. 12 Are not Abanah and Pharpar, the rivers of Damascus, better than all the waters of Israel? may I not wash in them, and be clean? So he turned and went away in a rage. 13 And his servants came near, and spake unto him, and said, My father, if the prophet had bid thee do some great thing, wouldest thou not have done it? how much rather then, when he saith to thee, Wash, and be clean? 14 Then went he down, and dipped himself'seven times in the Jordan, according to the saying of the man of God; and his flesh came again like unto the flesh of a little child, and he was clean.

Gehazi's Greed and Leprosy

15 And he returned to the man of God, he and all his company, and came, and stood before him; and he said, Behold now, I know that there is no God in all the earth, but in Israel: now therefore, I pray thee, take a present of thy servant. 16 But he said, As Jehovah liveth, before whom I stand, I will receive none. And he urged him to take it; but he refused. 17 And Naaman said, If not, yet, I pray thee, let there be given to thy servant two mules burden of earth; for thy servant will henceforth offer neither burnt-offering nor sacrifice unto other gods, but unto Jehovah. 18 In this thing Jehovah pardon thy servant: when my master goeth into the house of Rimmon to worship there, and he leaneth on my hand, and I bow myself in the house of Rimmon, when I bow myself in the house of Rimmon, Jehovah pardon thy servant in this thing. 19 And he said unto him, Go in peace. So he departed from him a little way.

20 But Gehazi the servant of Elisha the man of God, said, Behold, my master hath spared this Naaman the Syrian, in not receiving at his hands that which he brought: as Jehovah liveth, I will run after him, and take somewhat of him. 21 So Gehazi followed after Naaman. And when Naaman saw one running after him, he alighted from the chariot to meet him, and said, Is all well? 22 And he said, All is well. My master hath sent me, saying, Behold, even now there are come to me from the hill-country of Ephraim two young men of the sons of the prophets; give them, I pray thee, a talent of silver, and two changes of raiment. 23 And Naaman said, Be pleased to take two talents. And he urged him, and bound two talents of silver in two bags, with two changes of raiment, and laid them upon two of his servants; and they bare them before him. 24 And when he came to the hill, he took them from their hand, and bestowed them in the house; and he let the men go, and they departed. 25 But he went in, and stood before his master. And Elisha said unto him, Whence comest thou, Gehazi? And he said, Thy servant went no whither.

26 And he said unto him, Went not my heart with thee, when the man turned from his chariot to meet thee? Is it a time to receive money, and to receive garments, and olive yards and vineyards, and sheep and oxen, and men-servants and maid-servants? 27 The leprosy therefore of Naaman shall cleave unto thee, and unto thy seed for ever. And he went out from his presence a leper as white as snow.'

Gehazi, despite having been the man most trusted by the prophet Elisha, was tempted by greed and money and ended up with a curse that affected his generations. This is quite sad given that he might have ended up being one of the great prophets of his time. He had seen God's miracles manifest, but the earthly desires took hold of him and destroyed his purpose.

There are some members of the Clergy who use all sorts of chicanery and manipulations to get money from the congregants. They should understand that God is watching and shall reap what they sow. We all also know about the story of Sapphira and his wife, who wanted to swindle God of his treasury, and they both died as a result of this. Mark 8 vs 36 states: '***For what will it profit a man if he gains the whole world, and loses his own soul?'***

Materialism should not make us his believers stumble or forsake the values and teachings of the bible, as these can easily dissipate or vanish.

Acts 5 vs 1- 10 says:

1   **But a certain man named Ananias, with Sapphira his wife, sold a possession,**

2   **And kept back *part* of the price, his wife also being privy *to it*, and brought a certain part, and laid *it* at the apostles' feet.**

3   **But Peter said, Ananias, why hath Satan filled thine heart to lie to the Holy Ghost, and to keep back *part* of the price of the land?**

4   **Whiles it remained, was it not thine own? and after it was sold, was it not in thine own power? why hast thou conceived this thing in thine heart? thou hast not lied unto men, but unto God.**

5   **And Ananias hearing these words fell down, and gave up the ghost: and great fear came on all them that heard these things.**

6   And the young men arose, wound him up, and carried *him* out, and buried *him*.

7   And it was about the space of three hours after, when his wife, not knowing what was done, came in.

8   And Peter answered unto her, Tell me whether ye sold the land for so much? And she said, Yea, for so much.

9   Then Peter said unto her, How is it that ye have agreed together to tempt the Spirit of the Lord? behold, the feet of them which have buried thy husband *are* at the door, and shall carry thee out.

10 Then fell she down straightway at his feet, and yielded up the ghost: and the young men came in, and found her dead, and, carrying *her* forth, buried *her* by her husband.'

I am surprised that some clergy end up stealing and manipulating from their congregations, yet they can easily enquire of the Lord and start their own businesses. The Lord says in Deuteronomy 8:18 *'I am the one who gives you power to make wealth'*.

Chapter 5:

World Issues bigger than materialism

We live in a modern world that is characterised by poverty, strife, war and selfishness. There has been much coverage in the media of terrorist attacks by Islamic fundamentalists. This appears to have caused or exacerbated the rift between Christians and Moslems.

The 9/11 and 7/7 bombings that happened respectively in the United States of America and the United Kingdom as a result of Islamic militant action has led to some sectors of the communities in both nations harbouring a general hate towards Muslims. They also include some Christians. These were heinous crimes that were committed against ordinary citizens and they caused a lot of pain to the surviving communities and families. It is understandable that people would be upset and become more vigilant as a result of these incidents. A number of firemen died on duty in New York as they tried to put out the fire. These events have generated a lot of anxiety in the communities and made people hyper-vigilant. We need however to bear in mind that we should not let emotion and deep-seated misconceptions take advantage of us. Not all people of Islamic faith are terrorists, and the majority do not support the actions of, for example, the Islamic State. It is however important to note that some could be sympathetic and comply with the ideology of the Islamic State to create a caliphate within the Present Syrian and Iraq states.

Some commentators viewed these terrorist acts as an attempt to disrupt or hurt the capitalist system of the West. The Islamic terrorists view non-Muslims as kafirs or infidels
who deserve to die if they refused to convert. It has also been argued that the attempt to establish a

Caliphate was not essentially for religion but to control the oil fields and mining rights. The militia uses terror and execution, including crucifixion, to quell dissent and opposition.

We need to continue to pray for peace and love in the Land. God is our anchor and support. The greatest weapon that can be used to conquer any act of aggression is love. The Bible tells us that we need to love our enemies and forgive their trespasses. This would seem an insurmountable task, given the bombings and other incidents of mass murder. James 1vs 2 mentions that we should count it all as joy when we go through tribulations.

As Christians we need to continue to show love, have patience and pray for our Muslim neighbours, as this is the only way we can win them for our Lord Jesus Christ. It should be accepted that no sermon, however good and inspiring, will result in Muslims turning to God. Our lives should be a blueprint of our faith and should speak volumes about our beliefs. Love covers a multitude of sins.

Paul mentions in 1 Corinthians vs 13 that speaking in tongues would not be important if you did not show love towards one another. Our Lord Jesus Christ in Matthew 22, when asked by the Pharisees what would be the best commandment, said 'love your God with all your heart, soul and mind'. He also went further, to say 'love your neighbour'.

It is intriguing to note that some Christians across ranks have become anti-Islamic, and this has been met by a negative response from the Muslims. There is a need to continue to extend a handshake of love and peace to everyone. We are all the children of God, regardless of whether we are Israelites or Ishmaelites, Jews or Greeks, saved or unsaved. It also needs to be mentioned that Baroness Warsi, who was in David Cameron's government before she resigned, was instrumental in highlighting the plight of the Christians in the Middle East whilst some of our clergy have been mute and not championed the cause. As Christians, tolerance should be part of our everyday speech, and love should be our trademark and style.

The world we live in is full of vice, corruption, hatred and evil. When people do not show compassion and love towards us, it is not a licence for us to show revenge and animosity and abandon compassion.

Senator Robert Kennedy made a passionate speech in Philadelphia following the death of Dr Martin Luther King in Philadelphia in the United States, and his words remain relevant to this day now that we are faced with these Islamic fundamentalists who have caused so much confusion and chaos to our present day lives:

'For those of you who are black and are tempted to be filled with hatred and distrust at the injustice of such an act, against all white people, I can only say that I feel in my own heart the same kind of feeling. I had a member of my family killed, but he was killed by a white man. But we have to make an effort in the United States, we have to make an effort to understand, to go beyond these rather difficult times.

'My favorite poet was Aeschylus. He wrote: "In our sleep, pain which cannot forget falls drop by drop upon the heart until, in our own despair, against our will, comes wisdom through the awful grace of God."

'What we need in the United States is not division; what we need in the United States is not hatred; what we need in the United States is not violence or lawlessness; but love and wisdom, and compassion toward one another, and a feeling of justice toward those who still suffer within our country, whether they be white or they be black.

'So I shall ask you tonight to return home, to say a prayer for the family of Martin Luther King,

that's true, but more importantly to say a prayer for our own country, which all of us love – a prayer for understanding and that compassion of which I spoke.

'We can do well in this country. We will have difficult times; we've had difficult times in the past; we will have difficult times in the future. It is not the end of violence; it is not the end of lawlessness; it is not the end of disorder. But the vast majority of white people and the vast majority of black people in this country want to live together, want to improve the quality of our life, and want justice for all human beings who abide in our land.

'Let us dedicate ourselves to what the Greeks wrote so many years ago: to tame the savageness of man and make gentle the life of this world.

'Let us dedicate ourselves to that, and say a prayer for our country and for our people.'

This was one of Senator Kennedy's best speeches and he prepared it while he was travelling to address the people. What made this speech stand out is that he spoke about the need for compassion and love toward one another. We need to stick to our faith even in the face of difficult times and tempting situations.

This does not mean that we should be naive and not vigilant.

Matthew 10:16: '***Behold, I send you out as sheep in the midst of wolves; so be shrewd as serpents and innocent'***. Our Lord knew of the difficulties that we Christians were to endure in the world.

We also need to pray for the police and our army, that they will have the wisdom to combat terrorism and ensure safety to the public.

It is worth noting that Nelson Mandela, after serving 27 years in prison on Robben Island, did not show bitterness towards the white South African population but preached reconciliation and togetherness. He mentioned during the Rinovia trials that he had fought against domination by either white or black people and wanted a free South Africa for everyone.

It is also a biblical requirement that we should pray for Israel. This is despite our political persuasions or economic standing.

Chapter 6:

Radical Thinking: Who Says Who?

We should not apologise for sticking to our Christian faith, and we should not be dictated to by society about what we should or should not wear. As Christians we should not be coerced into buying things that we do not need just for the sake of fashion. At the end of the day, whose fashion? We serve a humble God who was born in a manger, next to sheep. This shows the humility of our God, that he did not choose to be born in a palace. His earthly parents were not wealthy or well known. Jesus Christ did not live a life of luxury; he dwelt amongst his disciples.

Who said that you need to divorce your husband or wife? Is it covetousness or lust?

Who says you need a new car, or a bigger one? Is it out of necessity, social pressure or ambition?

I have heard a number of friends and colleagues talk about houses and cars. I have heard people say, 'My car is better than his' or 'My house is bigger than hers.' The talk is driven by competition and envy. The Word tells us that we should not be envious of a neighbour's possessions or of his wife. Yet subconsciously, sometimes we end up acting as non-believers.

It is salient to note that we need to safeguard our minds and curb the battles that go in our heads. Joyce Meyer wrote an interesting book called *The Battlefields of the Mind*. In this book she explores the need to control our minds and ensure that the devil does not take hold of our thinking. The battle in the mind has to be won, otherwise we will continue to be slaves to fear and have fleeting thoughts. Everything is defeated or won in the mind.

We should not be impressionable and easily led, but be more Christ like. Jesus Christ could be seen or envisaged as a revolutionary of his time, as he brought a new belief dimension that was contrary to the Jewish tradition of the day.

It is imperative that we become humble and mind our own business, and not be envious or covetous. Our bible tells us that what a man thinks, so is he. It is important to continue to understand that any battle that we are facing is first won in the mind. Mental blocks, depression, anxiety and suicidal ideation come about as a result of not capturing the mind and the thinking processes. All our wild emotions and fleeting thoughts should be tamed and made subject to the obedience of the word.

Our mind is the oasis of our freedom. When the mind is liberated the whole human being is liberated, as well as the community. It is my view that a community full of sound-minded people is empowered in regard to progress and development.

William Cowper, the 18th century English poet, in his epic poem *Table Talk*, wrote: **'I will sing if liberty be there, and at liberty's dear feet'**. The essence of liberty of mind should not be underestimated.

A demon-controlled mind is subject to fear and despondence. This reminds me of the song 'I am not subject to fear', whose lyrics are:

You unravel me, with a melody

You surround me with a song

Of deliverance, from my enemies

Till all my fears are gone

I'm no longer a slave to fear

I am a child of God

From my mother's womb

You have chosen me

Love has called my name

I've been born again, into your family

Your blood flows through my veins

You split the sea

So I could walk right through it

All my fears were drowned in perfect love

You rescued me

So I could stand and sing

I am a child of God.

We need to pray for sanity and speak the word in our lives.

2 Corinthians 10:4 King James Version (KJV) states: **'For the weapons of our warfare are not carnal, but mighty through God to the pulling down of strongholds'**. It is salient that we wage war against the wiles of the enemy and capture any thoughts that

would affect our functioning. Lucifer is raging a war against Christians and wants to control their minds and thinking. That is why sometimes we end up putting much effort into things of this world and not focusing on God.

If we are not aware of Lucifer's wiles, he will devour and disempower us. This means that we need to remain steadfast in prayer and be sensitive in the spirit. Any evil spirits or occult launched by the enemy against us will not achieve their set purpose. Numbers 23v23 says: '***surely there is no enchantment against Jacob, neither is there divination against Israel: according to this time it shall be said of Jacob and Israel, 'what has hath God wrought?'*** It is a great panacea and encouragement that the Lord is our protector and deliverer and that he keeps and watches over His Word.

As children of God, we should not be complacent that the devil is there to kill and destroy. The bible refers to the devil as like the roaring lion looking for one to devour.

Isaiah 54v17 states: ***'No weapon that is formed against thee shall prosper and every tongue that shall rise against thee in judgement thou shall condemn. This is the heritage of the servants of the Lord, and their righteousness is of me, saith the Lord'***. No matter what difficult and trying situations we go through in life, it is important to remember that our Lord is our shield and providence.

Romans 8:6: ***"For to set the mind on the flesh is death, but to set the mind on the Spirit is life and peace."*** Clearly, we have many choices to make as human beings. We can choose to follow Christ, or we can do whatever makes us happy. However, this verse, written by the Apostle Paul, puts it all into perspective. Because the truth is that if we set our minds on our own desires and wants, then we will find only eternal death as our reward. But if we set our mind on God, His Holy Spirit brings us an amazing life now and forever that is full of hope and peace.

Chapter 7:

The Clergy and the Oaths of Serving

There has been a lot of publicity about men of the cloth not conducting themselves appropriately with other members of the congregation. Some pastors have been accused and even arrested for abusing male or female members of their congregations. These concerns apply to all churches across the board, regardless of colour or race.

I remember as a young person that there was a big hullabaloo when a certain evangelist was caught with a prostitute and this led the Church to defrock him. There is also a known pastor who made an out of court settlement with some young men who had made allegations against him of sexual and emotional abuse. He denied the allegations. We have also read about other pastors who have raped and sexually abused some members of their congregation. The list is endless, and some have been involved in financial scandals. In my native country, Zimbabwe, there has been a mushrooming of churches, and in some of these the gospel is being distorted and members of the congregation are being manipulated.

It needs to be emphasised that servants of God are there to serve and not to be served. They should be people of good moral standing and strength.1 Peter:5: 1-5 says: *'To the elders among you, I appeal as a fellow elder, a witness of Christ's sufferings and one who also will share in the glory to be revealed: Be shepherds of God's flock that is under your care, serving as overseers – not because you must, but because you are willing, as God wants you to be; not greedy for money, but eager to serve; not lording it over those entrusted to you, but being examples to the flock. And when the Chief Shepherd appears, you will receive the crown of glory that will never fade away. Young men, in the same way be submissive to those who are older. All of you, clothe yourselves with humility toward one another, because "God opposes the proud but gives grace to the humble".'*

This verse alludes to the fact that the pastors should be eager to serve and not greedy for money. Many times this has not been the case. Some of the clergy seem to see themselves as being above their congregation, and want to be served. They are usually accorded so much respect that it becomes difficult to challenge them or seek clarification on matters. In a nutshell, they end up being seen as demi-gods and in doing so they are depriving the Lord of the glory. All the glory should be to Yahweh, not man. In saying so, the congregation or parishes need to respect the anointing and the authority that has been endowed on the clergy by God. There needs to be order and respect in the house of God. The Pastors need to be approached with respect but not fear.

The need to put the leadership in check cannot be understated. In saying so, this is not to underestimate their role and functioning. The Apostle Peter, who was given the keys of heaven by Lord Jesus Christ, had to explain himself to his fellow believers and was challenged openly by Paul in the presence of other disciples. He did not take it to heart or feel challenged, but with humility he responded to them. Peter did not pull rank and say 'You know what folks, I am the one who was designated as the heir by Christ, so get over it'. His humility could only be provided by Grace.

It should also be pointed out that Jesus Christ always entertained questions and was ready to explain or respond to them. Any matters should however be raised with respect and humility, realising that the Pastor is the spiritual father of the house. If matters are raised and discussed in a cordial and brotherly way, this would make the church more responsive and increase their functioning.

The lack of inquisitorial and critical enquiry in churches or Christian circles can lead to grave and dire consequences. Some may have heard or read about the Guyana tragedy. This was when David Koresh, the leader of a religious sect called the Branch Davidians, manipulated and brainwashed his followers and told them they would go to heaven if they drank poison or cyanide with him. It is mortifying that this was an American church but that the congregants were overly persuaded and ended up in Guyana. Concerns were also raised that there may have been sexual abuse in the Church which went unmitigated and unreported.

Members of the church were threatened, and some ended up selling their property and forwarding the proceeds to the church.

There have also been videos on YouTube and the Internet of a certain pastor telling his congregants to eat grass as part of their deliverance. This is an anathema and quite contrary to the Gospel. Deliverance is based on a person acknowledging that Jesus Christ is the Lord and Saviour. There is no power or anointing in the grass, and this is cultic in manifestation.

Some church leaders have degraded or make mockery of the power of the Cross by selling so-called 'anointed oil' in bottles and telling their congregants that it will deliver them from evil spirits and demons. How can God's power be confined in a bottle of oil!

In 2014 there was a media frenzy in Zimbabwe when a certain pastor was arrested in Zimbabwe for raping and abusing women in the church. It is reported that he even boasted in front of the church, 'all the women in this church are mine'. It was also reported that he intended to sleep with every woman in the church.

We need to have praying and supportive elders in the church who are able to keep the leadership in check. It is a biblical requirement that men and women of the cloth are looked after and that they do not experience hardship or be abased. Deuteronomy 14 vs 27-29 stated: *'²⁷You shall not forsake the Levite who is within your gates, for he has no part nor inheritance with you.*

"²⁸At the end of every third year you shall bring out the tithe of your produce of that year and store it up within your gates. ²⁹And the Levite, because he has no portion nor inheritance with you, and the stranger and the fatherless and the widow who are within your gates, may come and eat and be satisfied, that the Lord your God may bless you in all the work of your hand which you do.'

We have heard sad stories or accounts of pastors who are living in absolute poverty or who have left the ministry due to financial hardships. It is important that pastors are provided for, so that they may fully focus themselves on the work of the ministry for which God has called them.

The early Church had a vision and was at the centre of society. It catered for the needy and the vulnerable. The Church was also involved in politics and was a vehicle for social justice and social change. It is imperative that the pastors preach the gospel of empowerment and bring back the church to the centre of societal influence. Pastor Derbyshire of City

Gates Elim Church, in one of his inspirational seminars, mentioned that the church building was being erected in the centre of Ilford, Essex as it needs to be relevant and be seen by the locals. This was the time when City Gates Church building was in the process of being built and the foundation was being laid down.

The Bible informs us that faith without works is dead. There is a book in the Bible called Acts which details the exploits of the Apostles. This depicts the incredible works that were performed by the Apostles following the outpouring of the Spirit, as written in Acts 2:1-4 v: *'When the day of Pentecost had fully come, they were all with one accord in one place. And suddenly, there came a sound from heaven, as of a rushing mighty wind, and it filled the whole house where they were sitting. Then there appeared to them divided tongues, as of fire and one sat upon each of them. And they were all filled with the Holy Spirit and began to speak with other tongues as the spirit gave them utterance.'*

The Apostles understood the importance of alms-giving and collectivisation in helping the poor. They, the congregants and the community pulled their resources together with a view to ensuring that no one went without in the church. Some believers and folks have termed this 'Christian socialism'. This is however debatable, as God and Jesus are not central to socialism as is influenced by dialectic thinking and sees religion as the alienation of man from rational thinking.

The sharing, as highlighted in the book of Acts 4 v32-37:

"[32]All the believers were one in heart and mind. No one claimed that any of their possessions was their own, but they shared everything they had. [33]With great power the apostles continued to testify to the resurrection of the Lord Jesus. And God's grace was so powerfully at work in them all [34]that there were no needy persons among them. For from time to time those who owned land or houses sold them, brought the money from the sales [35]and put it at the apostles' feet, and it was distributed to anyone who had need.

[36]Joseph, a Levite from Cyprus, whom the apostles called Barnabas (which means "son of encouragement"), [37]sold a field he owned and brought the money and put it at the apostles' feet.'

The purpose of sharing possessions was not to create an egalitarian society but to respond to need. This is different from seeking to establish an egalitarian society. Whilst an egalitarian society is desirable, it is impossible to establish this on earth through human effort. For those who have held themselves as Socialists such as the former Soviet Union, it is known that there was much class division, corruption and oppression.

Modern states in the world such as China and North Korea, who purport to practise communism, are characterised by general poverty and oppression. China has made progress in regard to economic development, but there has not been an effect on the economy. Some of the children of the Politburo were educated in the United States of America and the United Kingdom, at the same time championing equality, yet the majority were drenched and soaked in poverty and oppression.

The purpose of some social policies in the world, such as the Ujamaa Policy in Tanzania propagated by the late President Dr Julius Nyerere, and collectivisation under Chairman Mao Tse Tung and Josef Stalin in Russia, were focused on achieving equality and egalitarianism. Under these schemes people were forced off their land and most of them were never compensated. Quite a number of prosperous peasants in Russia, known as the Kulaks, were sent to prison in Siberia, tortured and executed.

This is different from Christian collectivism, where believers were under no compulsion to give but gave for common good and measure. The purpose was to look after the needy in the church and provide a safety net. We as believers are endowed with different gifts and some have been granted the entrepreneurial spirit and would financially prosper more than other. Our gifts should be used for the betterment of mankind and not for selfish and avarice purposes.

There are a number of vulnerable and needy families in the community and in the world that need our support, love and affection. It is estimated that there are about 40 million HIV/AIDS orphans living in Sub-Saharan Africa. The orphans are living in extreme poverty, and are marginalised and socially excluded. The poor economies of the developing countries on that continent and the overstretched family networks have reduced the assistance and the support that can be offered to them. The orphans live in different circumstances, and their situation is made worse because they are mostly not legally protected making their situation dire. General poverty has stood in the way of them and has resulted in some of them becoming street children, involved in prostitution, gangs and crime.

Many years ago, there was an incident in which the Brazilian police were accused of killing and maiming street children. This was carried out as a response to crime in the community.

There are many factors that have stood against these children. The children who are living in difficult circumstances are not meeting their milestones and living in environments that are unsafe and unpredictable.

It should be our purpose and our mission to champion people's rights and look after the disadvantaged in the community. Isaiah 1:17 states*: 'Learn to do good, seek justice, reprove of the ruthlessness defend the orphans and the widows and ensure their wellbeing'.* There is a need for more work or effort in this regard.

We have heard and read in the news about surviving children and widows whose inheritance is being siphoned off by avaricious and self-aggrandising relations.

The community and the church now seem to shy away of their responsibilities. It is our moral duty to protect the vulnerable and go beyond church walls to make a positive impact in the community. The church has to take a step to be at the centre or axis of transformation and morality. Political, economic and social policies have a salient part to play in improving the plight of the vulnerable and disenfranchised, but the spiritual cannot be put aside or side-lined to the margins when attempting to address the ramifications of the problems confronting us.

There are various ways in which we can assist the vulnerable children by meeting their physical, health, social, safety and emotional needs. Clothing is also one of the needs that need to be addressed.

Jesus Christ gave us the great mission to spread the word of God around the whole world. The Bible informs us that it is not the desire of God that people perish but that they should enjoy everlasting life. As Christians, we are expected to preach and explain the Good News to unbelievers for them to be served. In doing so we need to have the true spirit of God, with wisdom and courage. It is paramount for us to pray for boldness, just as the Apostles did in the book of Acts when they were being persecuted and faced with the Sanhedrin Council.

There is need to be cleverness and shrewdness when engaging with the public. People in marketing would inform you that it is easier to sell a product that you believe in. In the same vein, your attitude and belief will attract many conversions and believers.

The difference between Christianity and many other religions or belief systems is that conversion and believing are not forced, nor should people be under any compulsion. Jesus stated (Mark 6:11): 'If anyone will not welcome you or listen to you, shake the dust off your feet when you leave that place, as a testimony against them.' It is my assertion that Jesus Christ is the biggest democrat of all time. He brought a gospel that is based on voluntary engagement and not compulsion. We thus need to be conscious of this when we are evangelising. Temptation to use fear, manipulation or coercion to convert people must not be entertained.

There are various ways of sharing the word of God. They could include talking to aware neighbours and your workmates if they do not believe in salvation. It is also important to say that your lifestyle and conduct should speak about the Gospel in themselves. People should see Jesus Christ in your interaction, demeanour and everything you do at work. No vile or profane word should proceed from your lips. The glory that shone on Moses when he left Mount Sinai after speaking to God should be overtly evident on you. At work, people should see you as the conscience of your workplace and a moral figure.

It will be almost impossible for you to try to share

the good news if you are known in the community, at work and in your social circle as a philanderer, a drunkard or a party animal. The same applies to our neighbours. They should emulate our lives and see glory in everything we do.

Charity work is also an area that can be used to reach communities. It should always be remembered in our Christian walk that Jesus Christ responded to people's needs in his miracles. When five thousand people who were hungry came to see him preach, he fed them with two fishes and five loaves. He also raised Lazarus from the dead. Peter and John healed a paralytic and told him to rise up and walk, and he did so. Faith needs to be seen in action. The awesome ministry of Jesus Christ and his disciples was a healing ministry in its own right.

There are also opportunities to reach out to disadvantaged children across the world. This would include providing for HIV/AIDS orphans, street children and children involved in prostitution and vice. These children need our support, love and provision. It would not make sense for one to preach the Bible to a hungry child as her physical needs should be met first. I remember seeing some Christians preaching to children on the streets of Zimbabwe. What these children needed first was food and shelter. In saying this, I am not minimising the power of prayer and the Gospel but saying that we should always endeavour to be practical. Sometimes we use 'prayer' as an escape for not facing to the challenges confronting us. I have put the word 'prayer' in italics as some people use it as an easy way out. You hear them say 'don't worry, I have been praying for you'. This might not be the case. Prayer involves agony, self-denial, not just talk and pretence.

The Christian fraternity may also fulfil the great commission by donating to outreach programmes such as Operation Aaliyah in Israel, God channels and charity projects in their communities and home areas.

The Christians who are running risky underground Christian movements in areas such as Saudi Arabia and North Korea, where the Gospel is banned, need to be supported and provided with the support they require. We need to ensure and support the work of producing more bibles in different tongues and languages.

It is salient to highlight that the work that focuses on the Great Commission will be derailed if the Church does not come together and focus on the work before us. This means that any issues that relate to racism, tribalism and any form of discrimination in the church should be challenged and prayed against. There is danger that these ills will disable the vision and the talent in the church that should be focused on making a positive influence in the world.

Chapter 8:

Marriage and Christian Living

As Christians, we need to continue to respect the sanctity of marriage. Marriage is a God-ordained union where there is the physical and spiritual unity of a man and a woman.

There are now different definitions and forms of marriages in different societies and across countries, but our Bible only alludes to the union between man and woman.

Nowadays there are financial, social and family

pressures that exert much strain on marriage. I remember reading a newspaper article which highlighted the fact that one in three marriages in the United Kingdom results in divorce.

Society sometimes underestimates the importance that marriage plays in communities and societies; it brings stability to families and children. It has been reported that children who grow up in single-parent homes are more likely to be involved in crime. It needs to be emphasised that there are exceptions to the rule. Barack Obama, the former American President, and Hillary Clinton, the Secretary of State, both grew up in single-parent homes but went on to do extremely well and to become outstanding citizens in their own right. Social and environmental factors also need to be taken into account whilst making this assertion.

Despite bringing stability to individual families and society, marriage indicates great commitment and demands moral fibre. It represents tolerance, unity and common purpose. The importance of marriage cannot be overestimated, as it creates an environment of intimacy, safety and love. Bakare (2011) highlights the fact that marriage was created and designed for love and enjoyment, but that there are also tensions in it.

Marriage is defined by Kostenberger (2018) from

a Christian perspective as a sacred bond between a man and a woman instituted by and publicly entered into before God and normally consummated by sexual intercourse.

Genesis 2:24 stipulates: *'a man shall leave his father and mother and hold fast to his wife and the two shall become one flesh'*. There is also exclusivity in marriage and any sexual relations outside the institution are not permitted and are viewed as being perverse and sinful.   `

Cohabitation is different from marriage, as it is not secure and there is less commitment. Partners may just walk away when things get difficult or challenging. I have had some friends and relations stating that cohabitation is the new form of marriage. This is not the case. Some couples are now using cohabitation as a precursor to marriage, which can be described as 'let us enjoy ourselves and see what happens in the future'. I do not understand why some individuals who have been cohabiting for a long time are not keen to get married.

As Christians we need to protect and value the sanctity of marriage. It should always be at the back of our minds that God is against divorce and it was never his plan.

Marriage is not an easy institution, and couples should seek counselling and support when they get into difficulties. Throwing the towel should not be an easy option.

Research has also shown that children experience loss due to the divorce and separation of their parents. Some children have been reported to be withdrawn and to experience suicidal thoughts.

It is salient that as couples we pray together. Stormie Omartian, in her best-selling books *The Power of a Praying Wife* and *The Power of a Praying Husband*, highlights the importance of prayer. She mentions that her husband's prayers helped her to cope with her past and her anxieties. When one partner observes that the other is becoming spiritually weak, it is important to stand in the gap for one another. I have been married for 13 years and have come to the conclusion that marriage is like a field that needs to be cultivated and watered. If a field is not cultivated, the crops will be choked by the weeds. The corollary is that if marriage is not promoted and little time, effort and communication is invested in it, it will wither and die like a lily.

There are a lot pressures in the world that work against marriage, as mentioned above, including work, family and financial pressures. It is important that we make time to see one another and do not allow the devil to ruin our marriages.

Epilogue

Jesus Christ is looking for a loving, faithful bride with no wrinkles as stated in Ephesians 5:27. He desires intimacy and can only give this to a bride who does not commit to other gods. 'Wrinkles' in this context relate to us having wandered away from God and stopped following his will and law.

There is a danger of us putting too much importance on earthly things, which may lead us to end up idolising them. The current media can be likened to *Pravda*, the Russian newspaper, which has peddled lies with the purpose of controlling the minds and the movements of people.

It is important to bear in mind that all advertisements are there to influence our thinking so that we can part with our money and buy products. There is nothing wrong with desiring to have good things in life such as big cars and houses, but they cannot replace our Lord Jesus Christ and they fall short in fulfilling our emotional wellbeing. The Lord said, '*The thief does not come except to steal, and to kill, and to destroy. I have come that they may have life, and that they may have it more abundantly*'. He desires us to live abundantly and not lack anything. This however does not mean that we should live beyond our means or compete with each other. We should also not steal or be involved in illicit activities to sponsor our lives. The Bible also mentions that He does not withhold good things from his children.

We should not be fooled by the media into believing His non-existence or be coerced into sinning, for He is coming. No one knows the day, the time and the moon, but He is coming. Revelations 1Vs 7 states: '*7Behold, he cometh with clouds; and every eye shall see him, and they also which pierced him: and all kindreds of the earth shall wail because of him. Even so, Amen*'.

As Christians we need to continue to hold fast to our faith and not be moved. This is compounded by Hebrews 10:23, which states: *'Let us hold unswervingly to the hope we profess, for he who promised is faithful.'* Our faith means living right and not giving in to carnal desires but observing the statutes and laws of God. The Bible also tells us that the Christian journey is muddled with thorns and pain, but His Grace is sufficient for us.

Hebrews 13:8 tells us that Jesus Christ is the same yesterday, today and tomorrow. He does not change and his word is the blueprint for our current living.

The current preoccupation with material things and not looking unto God, the author and perfector of our faith, has compromised the power and the moral standing of the Church. We should never forget that material worth is temporary and that we do not take it to heaven. Material belongings are made for us to use, but they should not become a hindrance or caricature to our beliefs and Gospel.

It is important to bear in mind that we should always walk in humility and always look up to heaven. 'Finally, brethren, whatsoever things are true, whatsoever things are honest, whatsoever things are just, whatsoever things are pure, whatsoever things are lovely, whatsoever things are of good report; if there be any virtue, and if there be any praise, think on these things' - Philippians 4:8.

As Christians we are under siege and in the watchful eye of the public, but we should always find comfort and solace in the knowledge that the Lord is always protecting us and will never put us to shame. Over-consumerism should not sear our consciences, and its force and its chains should be fought against.God is always faithful and we should always exalt his name. We need to honour, revere and love him.

I close this book with the salutation from Jude vs 17-24: ' *17But, dear friends, remember what the apostles of our Lord Jesus Christ foretold. 18 They said to you, "In the last times there will be scoffers who will follow their own ungodly desires." 19 These are the people who divide you, who follow mere natural instincts and do not have the Spirit.*

20 But you, dear friends, by building yourselves up in your most holy faith and praying in the Holy Spirit, 21 keep yourselves in God's love as you wait for the mercy of our Lord Jesus Christ to bring you to eternal life.

22 Be merciful to those who doubt; 23 save others by snatching them from the fire; to others show mercy, mixed with fear—hating even the clothing stained by corrupted flesh.[f]

24 To him who is able to keep you from stumbling and to present you before his glorious presence without fault and with great joy – 25 to the only God our Savior be glory, majesty, power and authority, through Jesus Christ our Lord, before all ages, now and forevermore! Amen.'

Bibliography

The Holy Bible, King James Version

Bismark, T (2002) *The Kingdom in Motion,* Truebrand Publishing, Texas

Giddens, A and Mitchell, D (2000), *Introduction to Sociology*

Joyce Meyer, *The Battlefield of the Mind*, Warner Faith, New York, W.W Norton, London

Omartian, O (2001), *The Power of a Praying Husband*, Harvest House Publishers, Oregon

Warren, R (2003), *The Purpose Driven Life*, Zondervan, Michigan

Webber, M (2001), *The Protestant Ethic and the Spirit of Capitalism*, John Wiley and Sons Ltd, London.